2|19

Katherine Johnson

Katherine Johnson

by Ebony Joy Wilkins

Illustrated by Charlotte Ager

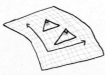

Editor Allison Singer
Senior Editors Satu Fox, Marie Greenwood
Senior Designer Joanne Clark

Project Editor Roohi Sehgal
Editor Radhika Haswani
Project Art Editors Radhika Banerjee, Yamini Panwar
Jacket Coordinator Francesca Young
Jacket Designer Joanne Clark
DTP Designers Sachin Gupta, Syed Mohammad Farhan
Picture Researcher Aditya Katyal
Illustrator Charlotte Ager
Senior Producer, Pre-Production Nikoleta Parasaki
Producer Basia Ossowska
Managing Editors Laura Gilbert, Monica Saigal
Deputy Managing Art Editor Ivy Sengupta
Managing Art Editor Diane Peyton Jones
Delhi Team Head Malavika Talukder
Creative Director Helen Senior
Publishing Director Sarah Larter

Subject Consultant Jamor Gaffney
Literacy Consultant Stephanie Laird

First American Edition, 2019
Published in the United States by DK Publishing
345 Hudson Street, New York, New York 10014
Copyright © 2019 Dorling Kindersley Limited
DK, a Division of Penguin Random House LLC
19 20 21 22 23 10 9 8 7 6 5 4 3 2 1
001–311577–Jan/19

A catalog record for this book is available from the Library of Congress.
ISBN: 978-1-4654-7912-9 (Paperback)
ISBN: 978-1-4654-7962-4 (Hardcover)

DK books are available at special discounts when purchased in bulk for sales promotions,
premiums, fund-raising, or educational use. For details, contact:
DK Publishing Special Markets,
345 Hudson Street, New York, New York 10014
SpecialSales@dk.com

Printed and bound in China

A WORLD OF IDEAS:
SEE ALL THERE IS TO KNOW

www.dk.com

Dear Reader,

Katherine Goble Johnson took control of her learning by questioning and pushing boundaries. As an African-American student in the 1920s and 1930s, she could have let the many roadblocks that had been set in her way stop her. Instead, she used them to drive her success. She had a team of family and knowledgeable mentors behind her, and with their support and her ambition, she soared.

Writing Katherine's story has inspired my own work, and when you read it, I hope it inspires you, too—to face fears, to work diligently, and to push for a fair place in this world. She's a role model, and she paved the way for many young scientists.

Katherine once said, "There's no such thing as a dumb question. It's dumb if you don't ask it." I'm going to accept that challenge and ask more questions as I pursue new goals. I challenge you to do the same.

Sincerely,
Ebony Joy Wilkins, PhD

The life of...
Katherine
Johnson

Counting ON KATHERINE

Katherine was born in 1918, in the town of White Sulphur Springs, West Virginia. Segregation was the law of the land.

During the 1800s, the government had decided that it was legal to separate people based on their race. African-American people were

forced to live and work in communities separate from white people. This separation meant that African-Americans could not be in the same schools, neighborhoods, churches, restaurants, buses or trains, or even hospitals with people of other races.

When Joshua McKinley Coleman and Joylette Roberta Lowe got married in 1909

SYSTEM OF SEPARATION

Segregation was a system that separated people of different races in many areas of life, including education. This practice kept black people down in society. Their schools, neighborhoods, and public transportation received less money than those for white people, and they were often paid less money for the same jobs.

in Danville, Virginia, segregation caused them to face a great many challenges. However, they were determined to fight for what they wanted, and despite these challenges, the Colemans had high hopes for themselves and their future. After moving to West Virginia in 1910, they took on various jobs around the tiny town of White Sulphur Springs.

To provide for the future family they wanted, Joshua took on jobs as a farmer, lumberman, janitor, handyman, and hotel worker. Joylette worked as a schoolteacher.

A few years later, their dream of having a family became a reality. The couple would end up having four children together. Horace, born in 1912, was the oldest Coleman child. Margaret was born a year later, in 1913, and Charles followed in 1915. Last, but not at all least, was Joylette and Joshua's youngest child, born on August 26, 1918—Katherine.

Both Joshua and Joylette believed that education was the key to survive and do well in life. Because of this, they encouraged their children to work hard and to achieve amazing things. For Katherine, this was easy from the start.

Joylette and Joshua recognized Katherine's love of numbers when she was very young. Even before she was old enough to go to school, Katherine had developed a talent for counting.

Katherine was envious when her three siblings started school before her. As the youngest, she had to wait her turn until her first day of school came, but she didn't waste any of this time. When Horace, Margaret, and Charles left for school each morning, Katherine followed them and counted their footsteps from the farm where they lived to the schoolhouse.

In fact, Katherine counted everything she could. Her family went to church together, and she counted the number of steps on the way there.

When it was her turn to help clean the kitchen after meals, Katherine counted the number of dishes, knives, and forks that she washed. When she played outside on the farm, she counted the number of steps to the road from home.

As she grew up, there were few things that Katherine didn't count. She became known in the community as the "little girl who loved to count," and Katherine herself once said, "Anything that could be counted, I did."

Because Katherine was so bright and curious as a child, those around her encouraged her to use her natural gift with numbers. Counting was her first love.

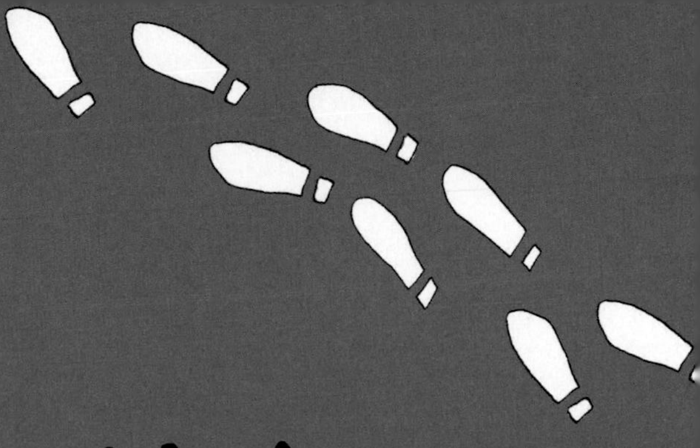

"Anything that could be **counted,** I did."

Katherine Johnson,
2015

13

Chapter 2

ASKING questions

After what felt like a very long wait, Katherine finally started school at age five. She could already count and read on her own.

Because of these skills, she was able to skip straight into the second grade. Skipping grades would turn out to be a pattern—Katherine did so well at school, she would later skip fifth grade, as well.

Her parents encouraged her to continue excelling at this quick pace, and they led by example. On the farmland the family owned, Katherine would watch as her father managed numbers while he worked. Even though he didn't go to school past the sixth grade, Joshua had a

DID YOU KNOW?

Katherine was good at many school subjects, but she has said that her worst was history.

natural talent for numbers.
He could calculate the amount
of wood one tree could
provide just by looking
at it. He could also help
Katherine solve some of
the math problems she
was given as homework.

Katherine learned
about teamwork and helping others
by watching her mother teach. In the early
20th century, most women were expected to
stay at home to raise children, and those who
worked outside of the home were usually
teachers or nurses. Joylette had become a
teacher, and she was passionate about her
work and her students.

Naturally smart and with excellent role
models at home, Katherine continued to do
well at school. It was no surprise to anyone in
her family when she was ready for high school
at only 10 years old, which meant she would be
learning alongside her older siblings.

Finding a high school where Katherine would be welcomed proved to be a challenge. Although she was ready for high school, high school wasn't exactly ready for her. There was a school for white children in White Sulphur Springs, but there was no high school available to African-American students. Katherine and her brothers and sister would have to either find somewhere else to continue their lessons, or stop going to school entirely.

Ending her schooling was not an option for Katherine. She loved learning too much, and her parents were too passionate about education to allow hers to end. They found a high school for black children in Institute,

West Virginia, on the campus of West Virginia State college—more than 100 miles (160 km) away from their home in White Sulphur Springs.

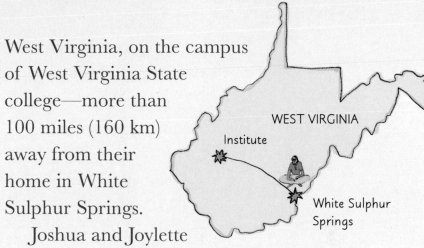

WEST VIRGINIA

Institute

White Sulphur Springs

Joshua and Joylette had to make a difficult decision, and they decided to make a sacrifice. Joshua would remain on the farm to continue his work while the rest of the family would move to Institute. Though the family would be apart during the school year, they believed it was worth it for the children's education.

The decision to move turned out to be a good one. Katherine continued to thrive. She found herself quickly conquering high-school level math. She was introduced to new subjects, too, many of which she liked.

what is sacrifice?

An action someone takes to give up something valuable for another person, or for the greater good.

But math always remained her favorite. "Everything is math," she once said. "It's just there. You're either right or you're wrong."

Despite her strong preference for math, Katherine had many talents. She studied French and learned to play the piano, an instrument she would one day help others learn, too. She also studied astronomy, the science of space.

There was a secret to Katherine's success: asking questions. In her classes, her hand was always in the air. Sometimes she would notice her classmates or siblings struggling during their lessons, and she would ask questions that she knew they were too shy to ask. Often they were questions she already knew the answers to, but she didn't mind. "There's no such thing as a dumb question," Katherine said. "It's dumb if you *don't* ask it!"

"There's no such thing as a **dumb question.** It's dumb if you **don't ask it!**"

Katherine Johnson, 2011

Katherine's high-school teachers noticed right away that she was a positive influence on her classmates. They began creating new classes specifically with Katherine in mind—like analytic geometry, which the school did not offer previously.

Two teachers in particular gave Katherine advice and watched out for her well-being. Her math teacher, Angie Turner King, was a very talented mathematician herself. She earned a PhD in math and chemistry by studying during the school's summer vacations. Katherine's other mentor was her high-school principal, Sherman H. Gus.

what is geometry? The math of shapes. Analytic geometry is an advanced type of geometry that uses sets of numbers called coordinates.

Mr. Gus would sometimes walk Katherine home from school. Along the way, he would point out the night sky's constellations, helping to grow Katherine's love of astronomy.

Both Dr. King and Mr. Gus encouraged Katherine to keep asking questions about the world. Together, they helped Katherine develop the curiosity that would serve her well for the rest of her life.

3

Separate AND unequal

Katherine graduated high school with honors at just 14 years old, and she was headed for college at 15.

Many students at her school got jobs after graduation—but Katherine had her sights set on a career in math, and she would need to

further her education to get it. She was just fine with that! Katherine looked forward to going to college, a goal her parents had always dreamed of for their children.

Colleges at the time were segregated, just like other schools. Katherine enrolled in West Virginia State, which was an all-black college then.

Some people believed that segregation of schools had a negative impact on students. Others, white people in particular, thought that segregation was necessary. Either way, Katherine was used to learning in schools for only black students, and she refused to let it concern her one bit.

Because she was such a math whiz, Katherine breezed through the courses offered to her. Her confidence, curiosity, and mind for math helped her learn at a fast pace.

West Virginia State opened in 1891. Today, nearly 30,000 students are enrolled there.

As always, Katherine helped her fellow students—and once again, her teachers took notice. When she had completed and mastered all of the math courses at West Virginia State by her third year in school, her professors created more advanced courses especially for her.

Her love of math was unwavering, and her professors began helping her think about what kind of career she might like. One professor, Dr. William W. Schieffelin Claytor, introduced

TOP-NOTCH TEACHER

Dr. Claytor taught at West Virginia State between 1933 and 1936. He was the third African-American to receive a PhD in mathematics, but he was prevented from having a successful career in research by racist attitudes that blocked his progress. Later, top researchers did want to hire him, but he had decided to devote his life to teaching students instead.

Katherine to the idea of working as a research mathematician. A research mathematician is someone who works to develop math theories and who looks for trends, or patterns, in sets of data. It may sound complicated, but as soon as she learned what the job was, Katherine was hooked. In this role, she would be able to put her math skills to use in real-world settings, instead of just at school. So it was decided: Katherine would be a research mathematician. Now she had a career path and a dream.

Unfortunately, there weren't many job opportunities for Katherine when she graduated from college in 1937. She was African-American and she was a woman,

which was not a good combination for the job market at the time. Employers were legally allowed to choose not to hire candidates like Katherine. The odds of her finding work, even with her college degree, were extremely unlikely.

Katherine kept her hopes up. She considered every opportunity that presented itself, including one she had expected: teaching. Katherine knew women were expected to work as teachers or nurses, or to stay home with children. She didn't have children yet, and she had always shown

an ability for teaching others. Right after her graduation from West Virginia State, she took a job as a high-school teacher in Marion, Virginia. There, she taught French, gave piano lessons, and helped with the student choir.

Katherine liked teaching her students, and she was good at it. However, soon a new opportunity would come up that Katherine never expected, one that would set her on the career path of her dreams.

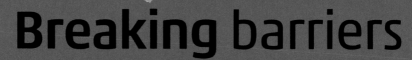

Breaking barriers

Katherine was teaching class one day in 1939 when the former president of West Virginia State, Dr. John W. Davis, approached her.

Dr. Davis had a new opportunity for her, one she hadn't seen coming. He knew Katherine had been interested in continuing her studies, but in the state of West Virginia, there were no graduate programs at black colleges. In the past, that would have meant Katherine's studies were over.

However, the year before, the US Supreme Court had ordered traditionally white colleges to open their doors to black students. This process of putting black and white students

What is the US Supreme Court?	The highest court in the United States. It is one of the three branches of government established by the US Constitution.

IMPORTANT RULING

In 1935, a black student named Lloyd Gaines applied for law school at the University of Missouri. He was denied entry because of his race. Because there was no similar school for black students nearby, the Supreme Court ruled that the university either had to create one or let him in.

into the same schools was called integration. The ruling would be life-changing for many people, Katherine included.

When the governor of West Virginia asked Dr. Davis for the names of three exceptional black students, Katherine made the list. She was accepted for the graduate school's summer session to study mathematics. As a parting gift, her boss at the high school gave her a set of reference books to help with her studies.

Katherine's mother moved in with her to help her adjust back into life as a student. She was also there for much-needed moral support. Being one of the first black students in a traditionally white school would not be easy. Katherine knew people might be hostile to her because of her race. She also knew that she would have to work harder than she had in her entire life.

Katherine would be going to school with white students for the very first time. Luckily, she didn't have to start this journey alone.

Two other African-Americans, Kenneth James and W. O. Armstrong, had been selected by Dr. Davis to attend the school, too. (A few years later, Kenneth James would become the first black student to earn a master's degree from West Virginia State. W. O. Armstrong would earn his master's degree one year later.)

It was tough on the three of them to be pioneers at West Virginia at a time when the work of white people was valued above that of African-Americans—and especially above the work of African-American women.

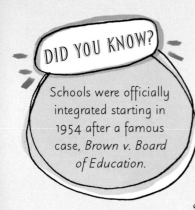

The integration of colleges was an important step in the fight for equality and fair treatment for students of all races. However, that didn't mean the change would be simple or easy.

In some schools and colleges, the first black students to attend what had been white-only schools had to arrive at school with a police escort. Some white families did not want African-American students there, so despite the new laws, there was a lot of tension. In some cases, there was violence.

INTEGRATION VIOLENCE

Bringing white and black students together to learn was not an easy task. Some white parents were not ready to see their children in an integrated school. They waved banners and screamed at black children who were trying to go to school. This was especially frightening because crowds of white people sometimes hurt or even killed black people.

Katherine had broken many barriers in her lifetime already. She'd skipped grades, mastered math at all grade levels, and graduated college early with the highest honors. In her new life as a graduate student, though, Katherine would have to prove herself all over again. Her very presence in West Virginia State's graduate program angered the people there who didn't believe in integration. Because of this, she wasn't able to focus only on her studies and building friendships. She also had to worry about her safety.

Many of her new classmates were nice to her, but some of the students were not friendly at all. Neither Katherine nor her classmates

were used to being in class with students of other races. The experience was new to everyone involved, including her professors. With that newness came uneasiness, and sometimes meanness. Some students and instructors discriminated against Katherine just because of her skin color. They thought that she couldn't and shouldn't learn in the presence of other students just because she had darker skin.

Despite any discomfort Katherine might have felt, she was glad to have her family's support. Her mother was close by to listen and to help Katherine when she needed her most.

With her mother's support, Katherine made the decision to succeed despite any harmful negativity that came her way.

Over the course of the summer session, Katherine's graduate school professors began to see how special her mind really was. Her math skills were beyond those of most of her classmates, and her attitude toward learning was inspiring.

Katherine was doing well at graduate school because, for her, excelling was the only option. For this reason, her professors began to treat her fairly and support her in her goals.

Chapter 5

A new journey

Katherine met and married James Francis Goble in 1939, the same year she began attending graduate school.

When the summer session was over, Katherine had a difficult decision to make. There was nothing she loved more than studying math and using her talents and skills to help others, but, now that she was married, Katherine was eager to start a family. Her parents had been hardworking and dedicated to their children. They had sacrificed much in order for Katherine and her siblings to have a good life. Katherine was willing to sacrifice for her future family, too—in this case, by leaving graduate school to focus on having and raising kids.

A little over a year after Katherine made her decision, she and James had their first child—a baby girl they named Joylette, the same name as Katherine's mother. They would have two more daughters—Constance and Katherine—in the years that followed.

In the early 1950s, once their children had grown from babies into young girls, Katherine and James moved their family to Newport News, Virginia. Once there, James began working as a painter at the Newport News shipyard and Katherine worked as a substitute math teacher while their daughters settled into their new schools.

The Newport News shipyard was founded in 1886 and is still active today.

Katherine adjusted well to her new life in Newport News. She and James worked hard at their new jobs, and they participated in the goings-on of the community. Katherine was known in several social circles as well as in her church for her service to her neighbors, and she developed a close, supportive circle of friends.

Katherine was also a member of Alpha Kappa Alpha Sorority, one of the first organizations for black women. She and the other women in this group focused on advocacy and social change. Katherine especially advocated for better education for African-American children, a cause both she and James strongly believed in.

what is advocacy? Publicly supporting a certain person or group, often with the intention of raising money or convincing others to join the cause.

ALPHA KAPPA ALPHA

A sorority is a society of people, typically female college students, who come together to socialize and advocate for causes. Katherine's sorority, Alpha Kappa Alpha, has more than 1,000 chapters across the country.

Although Katherine liked her new life in Newport News, she still dreamed of something more. She had fulfilled her dream of having a family, but she had not yet fulfilled her dream of becoming a research mathematician.

Then one day in 1952, her brother-in-law told her about an unusual newspaper advertisement he had seen. The National Advisory Committee for Aeronautics (NACA) had placed an ad calling for women to apply for jobs at Langley Research Center in Hampton, Virginia.

The ad read, "Reduce your household duties! Women who are not afraid to roll up their sleeves and do jobs previously filled by men should call the Langley Memorial Aeronautical Laboratory."

Katherine had never been afraid to work hard. She knew this might be her chance.

"Women who are not afraid to roll up their sleeves...should call the **Langley Memorial Aeronautical Laboratory.**"

1952 newspaper advertisement

Woman at work

The 1952 newspaper ad calling for women workers was unusual, but it would have been even more unusual 11 years earlier.

In 1941, President Roosevelt had declared that discrimination in the workplace was no longer allowed. This declaration happened partly as a result of World War II. While many men were off fighting in the war, women were needed to take on jobs at home that men usually did.

Despite President Roosevelt's declaration, many companies and organizations were still not willing to hire women, even by the 1950s. However, some did choose to open their doors to women, many for the first time.

| What is discrimination? | The practice of treating one person or group of people worse than others based solely on their race, gender, or other attribute. |

NACA was one of those organizations— and, even better, they were allowing African-American women to apply, too. This gave talented specialists like Katherine a long-awaited opportunity to further their careers.

NACA's Langley Research Center was a government agency in Hampton, Virginia, that conducted research on flying technologies, flight safety, and airplane designs.

Flight had been a crucial area of research during World War II. World leaders understood that the countries with the most airplanes would win the war. Airplanes did many important jobs—they carried soldiers and supplies, helped the military keep track of where the enemy was, and dropped bombs during battle. By 1943, the United States had three times the number of airplanes Germany had.

The war had been over for seven years when Katherine first learned of Langley's newspaper

FLYING TO WIN

During World War II, bombers, fighters, and transport planes were made that were bigger, better, and faster than ever before. The Allies' mighty air power helped them win the war. This type of American aircraft was often used by the Allied powers.

Curtiss P-40E Warhawk

ad in 1952, but flight research was still going strong. Katherine was happy as a math teacher, but she was excited for the opportunity to put her math skills to use as a research mathematician in this critical area.

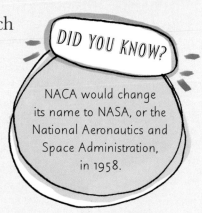

DID YOU KNOW?

NACA would change its name to NASA, or the National Aeronautics and Space Administration, in 1958.

Katherine applied for the position, but she was too late—the jobs had already been taken. Never one to give up, Katherine kept her eyes open for another opportunity to apply.

The next year, Katherine got her next chance, and this time she was successful! She started working for NACA in 1953, in the organization's Guidance and Navigation Department.

Katherine was hired to be a "human computer." This meant she would calculate data and analyze information for the male

BEGINNING OF COMPUTERS

In the early 1940s, engineers in the United States had begun designing a machine that could be programmed to solve math problems. It was called the ENIAC (the Electronic Numerical Integrator and Computer). It was the first modern computer. Over time, computers would become much smaller and more efficient.

engineers at Langley. The work, which desktop computers would do in later years, had to be done by hand at the time.

In an interview on television in 2011, Katherine described the work she did: "You had big data sheets, with maybe 15 or 20 columns across and 25 lines down, and

you solved those all the way across for days.
It was fascinating."

Katherine was part of a team of 12 African-
American human computers, all female research
mathematicians. They included Mary Jackson,
who worked on a supersonic pressure tunnel
project, and Dorothy Vaughan, who became
the first African-American manager at Langley.

The 12 women worked well together. They
calculated new technological advances and
flight-experiment data. The women built strong
friendships in the office, and they enjoyed one
another's company outside of work, too.

Katherine worked on math calculations with a pool (group) of women. She once called them "computers who wore skirts."

The human computers would often be asked to work on "special projects," where they would shadow the engineers as they did their research, then calculate and analyze the engineer's data.

After only two weeks on the job, Katherine was given her first special project. It was for the Maneuver Loads Branch. She researched data from flight tests and investigated the math behind plane crashes that were caused by turbulence. She did so well on the project, she was asked to keep working for the division. Katherine spent the next four years there.

During her time at Langley, Katherine earned a reputation as being someone who often spoke up and asked questions. "The women did what they were told to do," she said. "They didn't ask questions or take the task any further. I asked questions. I wanted to know why."

what is turbulence?

When a flying aircraft experiences sudden, violent movements because of changes in the air.

Katherine's years of studying had prepared her well for her role at Langley. Her dream of using her math skills for her career was finally coming true—she'd set her goal, and now she was achieving it!

Unfortunately, there was sadness in her life, too. In December 1956, Katherine's husband became very sick and died. Katherine was left alone with her three daughters, all of whom were in high school. Thanks to her work, she was still able to support her family.

Katherine poses for a portrait in Hampton, Virginia, in about 1960.

Chapter 7

Pushing for change

Although Katherine and her female coworkers were allowed in the workplace, some things had not changed.

The human computers were considered sub-professionals, which meant their work was thought of as a level below the engineers'. They were looked down on by the men, and they were required to work and eat separately. Katherine tried not to let the tension caused by the working conditions slow her down.

While she excelled at Langley, Katherine kept thinking about how to improve access and fair treatment for others. She was hardworking and dedicated to equality in the workplace for people of all races and genders.

DID YOU KNOW?

Katherine wrote a report on orbital flight. It was the first report in her division written by a woman.

There were a lot of rules about what African-Americans couldn't do. There were also a lot of rules about what women couldn't do. Katherine wanted to know why the rules were there in the first place. She also wanted to make room for future generations of scientists who would come after her.

Katherine's assignment was to calculate. She loved doing this, but in order to do her job better, she needed to learn what the engineers were learning. Katherine was determined to work more closely with the engineers, but some of the men didn't believe Katherine should be included in their meetings.

"I asked
questions.
I wanted to
know why.
They got used
to me...being the
only woman
there."

Katherine Johnson,
2013

No woman had ever attended these meetings before. No woman had even asked to attend the meetings before.

Katherine was persistent, and she would not take no for an answer. She questioned the people who told her that she couldn't participate, and she stood up for herself by asking if there was a law that kept her out of the meetings. There wasn't—and Katherine became the first woman to go to them.

Later in her life, when Katherine was asked about going to the meetings, she said, "They got used to me being the only woman there." She soon was known among the engineers for her extensive knowledge of geometry, her leadership skills, and her inquisitive nature.

Although they had been unsure at first, the engineers were impressed by Katherine's contributions to the meetings. They started trusting her to ask the right questions and to come up with strong solutions. They could see she didn't just follow directions—she always wanted to know more.

Meanwhile, Katherine's personal life took a happy turn. The pastor of her church in Newport News introduced her to Lieutenant Colonel James A. Johnson, a Korean War veteran. Later, in 1959, the two would get married.

Back at Langley, because she had gained the trust of her male colleagues, Katherine was called upon to work on several special projects. One of those projects gave her the chance to contribute equations to a report called "Notes on Space Technology."

---

what is a lieutenant colonel?

A senior officer in the US Army, Air Force, or Marines.

"Notes on Space Technology" included a collection of lectures assembled by engineers from NACA's Flight Research Division and Pilotless Aircraft Research Division. Of the many people who contributed to this important report, Katherine was the only woman.

After the report came out in 1958, some of the engineers who worked on it were asked to join a special task force called the Space Task Group. Engineer Dr. Robert Gilruth was appointed the group's leader.

Katherine was asked to be part of the Space Task Group as well. Being put on this project was a momentous occasion in her life. She had already made contributions to "Notes on Space Technology." Soon she would make even more contributions to space travel—ones for which people all over the world would one day recognize her.

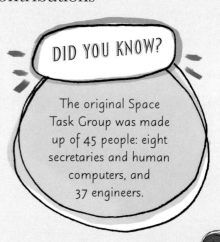

DID YOU KNOW?

The original Space Task Group was made up of 45 people: eight secretaries and human computers, and 37 engineers.

In the late 1950s, the United States was locked in a heated competition with another country—the Soviet Union. Katherine would play a role in helping to put the United States in the lead of that competition.

It was the country's biggest race to date, and it was called the Space Race.

This was the entrance to the headquarters of the Space Task Group at NASA.

Maxime Faget (second from right) was another member of the Space Task Group. Here, he examines a spacecraft model with coworkers.

Robert Gilruth (second from left) led the Space Task Group. He was a space pioneer who became the first director of NASA's Manned Spacecraft Center. This photograph is from August 1960.

The Space Race

In 1958, the Space Race between the United States and the Soviet Union (now Russia) was getting intense.

The year before, in 1957, the Soviet Union had sent *Sputnik 1*, the first artificial satellite, into space. Now both countries were racing to be the first to send an aircraft operated by a human into space. The pressure was on.

NACA was determined to be the first to accomplish the task. To prove this, in 1958, NACA became NASA, which stands for the National Aeronautics and Space Administration.

As part of NASA's newly formed Space Task Group, Katherine was asked to work on the first program to put a human

NASA's 1958 logo

in space. It was called
Project Mercury.

Project Mercury
had three goals: to send a
human-operated aircraft
into orbit around the Earth;
to study how the human body
reacts to being in space; and to safely bring
both the aircraft and the astronaut home.

Katherine's contribution to the project
would be to calculate launch windows. A launch
window is the exact moment when a spacecraft
needs to take off to reach space.

Figuring out when these windows would
happen was not an easy job. Katherine had to
determine the right launch speed of the aircraft,
its speed through the air, its direction, and the
landing spot it would come back to. One small
mistake in the calculations could cause the
whole mission to fail.

Katherine had spent her whole life so far
preparing for this, and because of her excellent
past performance, the engineers building the

spacecraft trusted her with the trajectory calculations. She knew the stakes were high. She would not let them, or herself, down.

However, the Soviets were one step ahead. In 1961, Soviet pilot Yuri Gagarin became the first person to travel into space and orbit the Earth. He went into space in the Vostok 1 spacecraft and spent one hour and 48 minutes there before parachuting back to Earth.

Just one month later, on May 5, 1961, the United States was ready to put Project Mercury into action by sending its first human-operated mission into space.

what is a trajectory?

The path an object follows through space. When you throw a ball, the path it takes through the air is its trajectory.

Katherine handled the trajectory analysis for the flight. Trajectory analysis was critical to the success of the mission and the safety of the astronaut. It was about where the spacecraft would land and how it would get home. Alan Shepard, the astronaut who would be going on the mission, was confident that Katherine's math would get him into space and back home again safely.

Alan Shepard

The atmosphere was tense on the day the mission launched. The Mercury-Redstone 3 rocket would carry Shepard into space in the *Freedom 7* capsule. After a long wait, Shepard was blasted 116 miles (187 km) up through the atmosphere. He had become the first American in space.

The Mercury-Redstone 3 rocket launches from Cape Canaveral on astronaut Alan Shepard's Freedom 7 mission into space.

63

Shepard's journey was an amazing mission for Katherine to have been part of. Because of the mission's success, Katherine was assigned to work on important data for another flight in 1962. This time, the plan was to send a human-operated spacecraft around the Earth, as the Soviets had done with Yuri Gagarin.

Astronaut John Glenn would be going on this mission. He knew how important accurate calculations were. By this time, a computer was available to electronically calculate the mission, but Glenn didn't trust the machines to be accurate. They often made mistakes—it was still the early days of computing.

JOHN GLENN

John Glenn was one of the Mercury Seven, the seven pilots competing to be the first-ever astronauts. He was chosen to pilot the Mercury-Atlas 6 on America's mission to send a human into orbit.

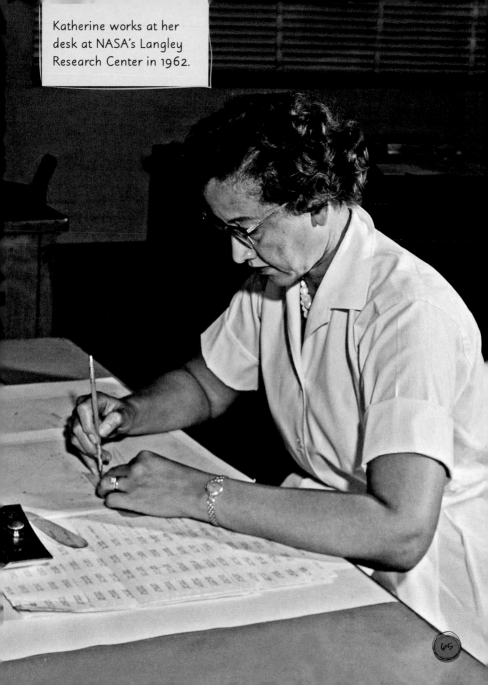

Katherine works at her
desk at NASA's Langley
Research Center in 1962.

Instead, John Glenn trusted a different kind of computer: a human one named Katherine. The astronaut requested that Katherine check the machine's numbers for his flight trajectory, to make sure they were absolutely correct. She knew that if the machine's calculation was off by even just a few seconds, it could mean the astronaut would be trapped in space. Katherine worked quickly, checking each number using her desk calculator.

When John Glenn heard that Katherine had double-checked the trajectory, he said, "If she says they're good, then I'm ready to go."

The flight was successful, and John Glenn became the first American to orbit the Earth. He made it back home safely—thanks in part to Katherine's accurate calculations.

DID YOU KNOW?

The first living creature to orbit the Earth was a dog named Laika, sent up by the Soviet Union in 1957.

The US had finally caught up to the Soviet Union in the Space Race.

The rivalry between the Soviet Union and the United States was far from over. Both countries had sent a person into space and around the Earth. Both countries had also sent artificial satellites, with no people onboard, to the moon. However, neither country had yet managed to get a person on the moon. This was the next challenge for Katherine and NASA, and it was a challenge that had been set by President John F. Kennedy himself.

---

what is rivalry?   An intense competition between two people or groups of people.

JOHN F. KENNEDY

John F. Kennedy, also called "JFK," was the 35th president of the United States. One of his favorite projects was the idea of putting a man on the moon. Sadly, he was assassinated before he was able to see his dream become a reality.

Back in 1961, on May 25, President Kennedy had made a speech before Congress. In it, he had announced his ambition of "landing a man on the moon and returning him safely to the Earth" before the end of the 1960s. He knew it would not be an easy feat to achieve. "In a very real sense," he said, "it will not be one man going to the moon...it will be an entire nation. For all of us must work to put him there."

With the success of missions like Alan Shepard's and John Glenn's, Katherine and her colleagues at NASA had the right experience and lots of confidence. They were ready to do what President Kennedy had asked and send a man to the moon.

"...it will **not be one man** going to the **moon...** it will be an **entire** nation."

John F. Kennedy, 1961

69

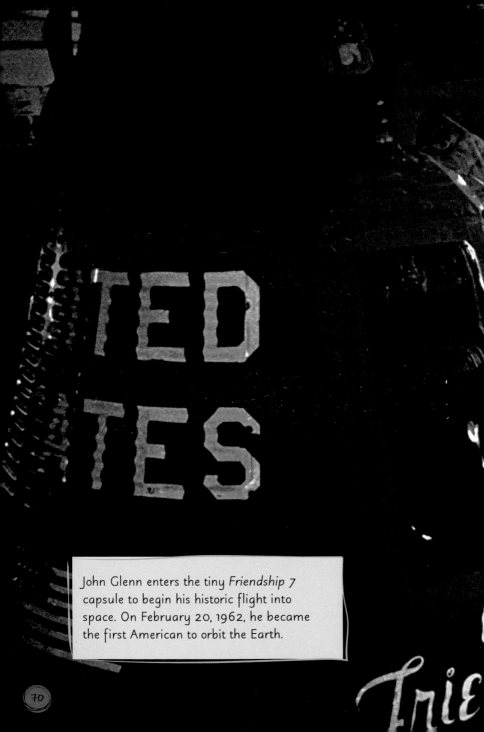

John Glenn enters the tiny *Friendship 7* capsule to begin his historic flight into space. On February 20, 1962, he became the first American to orbit the Earth.

dship

71

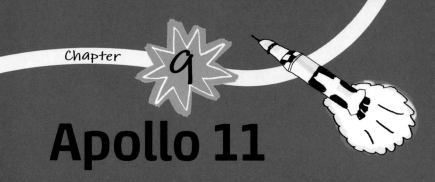

9

Apollo 11

If all went according to plan, Apollo 11 would be the first spacecraft with humans on board to land on the surface of the moon.

The three men chosen for this unique journey were highly trained and experienced. They were Edwin "Buzz" Aldrin Jr., the lunar module pilot; Michael Collins, the command module pilot; and Neil Armstrong, the mission's commander.

Each of the Apollo 11 astronauts had special assignments. The plan was for Collins to stay in orbit around the moon while Armstrong and Aldrin went to the moon's surface. Once on the moon, Armstrong and Aldrin would exit their craft. They would use cameras to take pictures of the landscape, as well as television cameras to send signals back to Earth.

COURAGEOUS CREW

Meet the three crew members of Apollo 11:

1. **Neil Armstrong** was born in Wapakoneta, Ohio, in 1930. He was a successful pilot in the US Navy, and he joined NACA in 1955.

2. **Michael Collins** was born in Rome, Italy—where his father, a US Army major general, was stationed in 1930. He was an experimental flight test officer in the US Air Force, then joined NASA in 1963.

3. **Edwin "Buzz" Aldrin Jr.** was born in Montclair, New Jersey, in 1930. He was a pilot in the US Air Force before joining NASA in 1963.

Armstrong and Aldrin would also collect lunar materials to bring back to Earth with them for further study.

Katherine and her team's main task was to calculate the trajectory for the journey to the moon. They were also responsible for figuring out backup navigational charts for astronauts in case of electronic failure.

Katherine needed to anticipate every move the astronauts would make. She would be told where they would launch from and where they should land, but the rest was up to her and the team. Every possible problem that might arise had to be thought about. The new computing machines would help, but they made mistakes. If Katherine didn't catch mistakes, the astronauts' lives would be in danger.

what are lunar materials?   Minerals and rocks found on the moon's surface.

Katherine worked tirelessly. She kept to a tough schedule of 14- or 16-hour days and worked many late nights. Katherine kept such long hours and was so absorbed with making sure the astronauts were kept safe that one day, on her way to work, she fell asleep while driving her car. Luckily, she woke up on the side of the road—shaken, but unhurt.

Mission Control appreciated the work of Katherine's team. Their calculations would help guide the spacecraft to the moon.

MISSION CONTROL

The Mission Control room at the Manned Space Center (now called the Johnson Space Center) was in Houston, Texas. Here, scientists and engineers would keep an around-the-clock watch of the spacecraft and talk to the crew over radio.

Blast off! On the morning of July 16, 1969, the launch vehicle for the Apollo 11 mission takes off at Cape Kennedy, Florida.

After many long days at the office, Katherine and the rest of the team's hard work was put to the test. On July 16, 1969, at 9:32 a.m., the Saturn V launch vehicle for the Apollo 11 spacecraft launched from Cape Kennedy (now called Cape Canaveral) at the Kennedy Space Center in Florida.

Hundreds of millions of people all over the world were glued to their TV screens, waiting to see what would happen next.

Spectators watch the Apollo 11 launch at Cape Kennedy. Some people traveled from across the country to witness the incredible event.

Chapter 10

"One **giant** leap"

The three astronauts sat in a tiny capsule at the top of the Saturn V rocket as it blasted into space from the Kennedy Space Center.

After that, a series of precise events took place, each carefully calculated by Katherine and her colleagues on the ground. First, the Saturn V rocket's engines fired to send the spacecraft out of the Earth's orbit. Then the command and service modules separated from the rest of the craft, rearranged themselves, and reconnected, ready to continue on to the moon. The rest of the rocket fell away, and the Apollo 11 spacecraft began its journey.

The entire way there, the astronauts kept their eyes on the numbers Katherine and her colleagues had carefully calculated. On July 17, their second day in space, Michael Collins took

SATURN V ROCKET

The Apollo 11 astronauts were sent into space inside the launch rocket Saturn V. The Apollo spacecraft was just the top part of the craft. It had three main areas: the command module, service module, and lunar module.

Escape rocket, for emergencies during launch

Apollo spacecraft

Command module, where the astronauts stayed during launch

Service module, which powered the spacecraft once it separated from Saturn V

The bottom part of Saturn V lifted the Apollo 11 craft into space.

Lunar module (called the *Eagle*), the part that would land on the moon

star sightings to compare their calculated flight path to their actual one. This means he looked to see what stars were visible and where they were, then compared them to what he would have expected to see if they were on track. Finding they were off, he fired the engine for three seconds to correct the trajectory. The astronauts trusted the numbers Katherine had checked and rechecked. They knew they needed to stay as close to them as possible.

JOURNEY TO THE MOON

Apollo 11's planned flightpath from the Earth to the moon and back again took the shape of a figure eight.

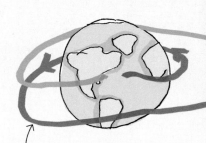

1. The Apollo craft leaves the Earth's orbit and begins its journey to the moon.

Back on the ground, the world continued to be fascinated by the mission. On July 18, their third day in space, the crew transmitted a 96-minute guided tour of their spacecraft back to Earth. It was broadcast live on television. People watched, awed by what they saw.

The journey to the moon took 102 hours, 45 minutes—just over four days. Once the spacecraft was in lunar orbit, Collins stayed in the command module while Armstrong and Aldrin entered the *Eagle*, or the lunar module, and took it to the moon's surface.

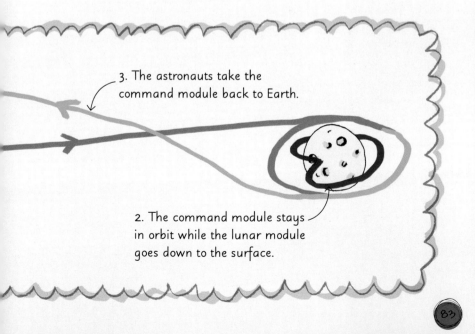

3. The astronauts take the command module back to Earth.

2. The command module stays in orbit while the lunar module goes down to the surface.

Mission Control gave the final go-ahead for the lunar module to land on the moon's surface. Then Armstrong used a fine-guidance controller to throttle the descent engines while Aldrin checked the module's altitude (height) and fuel. Both astronauts stared out of the windows, looking for a smooth area to land.

The *Eagle* needed a smooth landing. If it got too banged up, it might not be able to go back to the command module later.

The astronauts soon realized they were going to be landing several miles away from their calculated target. As the craft headed for a dangerous field of large boulders, Armstrong took manual control. He spotted a smooth plain and eased the craft down there instead, landing on the plain's surface with barely 20 seconds of descent fuel remaining. When the astronauts arrived safely, Armstrong famously said, "The *Eagle* has landed."

The world watched, mesmerized by what they saw next on their television screens.

SEA OF TRANQUILITY

The astronauts chose the Sea of Tranquility as their landing site. This is one of the several large, dark plains, called lunar mares, on the moon's surface. They were first called "seas" by early astronomers who mistook them for actual seas.

DID YOU KNOW?

The moon has only one-sixth of Earth's gravity, but the astronauts found moving around easier than expected.

The astronauts had made it to the moon! It was an amazing achievement and a historic moment. Neil Amstrong stepped out onto the moon's surface first, with Buzz Aldrin following closely behind him.

Armstrong and Aldrin planted the United States flag together. There is no wind on the moon, so the flag was held upright with wire to keep it from drooping. Work back at NASA was all but forgotten as the controllers turned from their desks to watch pictures of the first moon landing. One man's small step was the product of years of planning by a team of thousands. The live broadcast of the event caught the world's imagination in a way that has rarely been matched.

Armstrong and Aldrin were on the moon for over 21 hours. They spent about two and a half of those hours outside the *Eagle* walking, collecting lunar materials and data, and taking photos.

Buzz Aldrin walks on the moon's surface. You can see Neil Armstrong, who took the photograph, reflected in Aldrin's helmet visor.

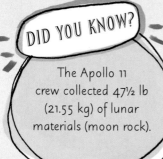

DID YOU KNOW?

The Apollo 11 crew collected 47½ lb (21.55 kg) of lunar materials (moon rock).

Their mission wouldn't be complete until they made it home safely—and whether or not that happened depended on how accurate Katherine and her team's calculations were. The crew needed to follow their instructions exactly to complete their planned splashdown, or water landing, in the Pacific Ocean. If they didn't, it could mean disaster.

Soon Armstrong and Aldrin were ready to return. They left behind the lower section of the lunar module, blasting off in the top section to meet Collins in the command module. This was a success, and together the three astronauts began their journey home.

When the command module had traveled back into Earth's atmosphere, three parachutes opened out to slow it down on its way toward the Pacific Ocean. The crew landed at 12:50 p.m. on July 24, 1969, about 13 miles (21 km) from the *USS Hornet* recovery ship, which was waiting to welcome them home. This was within the acceptable range Katherine and her colleagues had determined.

The mission had taken eight days, three hours, 18 minutes, and 35 seconds—but really, it had taken much longer. Katherine and many others had worked for years on this project, and now the Space Race was won. Katherine had never stopped believing that the mission to the moon was possible. She said, "You have to expect progress to be made," and indeed it had.

The command module bobs in the Pacific Ocean as the Apollo 11 astronauts wait for a helicopter from the *USS Hornet* recovery ship to retrieve them.

Buzz Aldrin stands by the United States flag he and Neil Armstrong had planted on the moon.

11

An **incredible career**

Getting the first man on the moon with Apollo 11 may be Katherine's most noted mission, but it wasn't even close to her last.

In fact, she worked on nearly every mission that followed at NASA while she was with the organization. Most of her time was spent creating backup plans for the computer systems. She knew that the computers weren't perfect, and that they could sometimes fail. She also knew that human error could occur. Katherine refused to let either of these potential issues jeopardize NASA's goals. She dedicated her skills to ensuring the safety of the astronauts who went on their missions.

what is human error?	A mistake made by a person that causes the results of something to be wrong.

That dedication paid off in 1970 when the Apollo 13 mission experienced malfunctions while in space. The three astronauts on board were in serious danger as they dealt with an oxygen tank that had exploded, damaging many of the aircraft's important systems. Thanks in part to the critical work Katherine did calculating and perfecting backup plans, the mission was able to return safely home.

APOLLO 13

The three Apollo 13 astronauts (from left to right: Fred Haise, Jim Lovell, and Jack Swigert) returned safely after their unsuccessful mission.

Besides working on backup plans, Katherine spent a lot of time writing for NASA. At one point, the members of the Space Task Group were asked to write a space-travel textbook. The information they were discovering was brand-new, so it had never been written about before.

The engineers on the task force had other responsibilities and projects, and they were concerned the textbook would not be completed by its due date. Katherine saved the day by offering to finish it herself. The engineers trusted her to do the work, and to do it well—which, of course, she did.

The space-travel textbook was only one of the many writing contributions Katherine made to NASA. She also authored or co-authored scientific research papers on many important topics.

SPACE TRAVEL

The papers explained the task force's research in areas such as the proper angles for satellites orbiting the Earth, how those satellites were expected to behave, space antennas, and more.

While at NASA, Katherine became a mentor to many people. Although her work kept her busy, sometimes extremely so, she always made time to teach others. She encouraged her coworkers to ask difficult questions, as she herself had always done. She also helped inform them about the programs that were happening at Langley.

Her coworkers weren't the only ones who benefited from her mentorship. As dedicated to education as ever, Katherine also took the time to mentor young mathematicians. She visited students in classrooms across the country to represent NASA and the Space Task Group.

DID YOU KNOW?

Katherine authored or co-authored about 26 research reports during her career at NASA.

During her school visits, Katherine encouraged students to follow in her footsteps by pursuing degrees and careers in STEM fields.

When Katherine retired from NASA in 1986, she had worked at the organization for an incredible 33 years.

"I loved going to work every single day," she later remembered. Her love of her work paid off. During her years of service, Katherine won three NASA Special Achievement awards.

STEM SUBJECTS

STEM is the grouping of four subjects (science, technology, engineering, and mathematics). It shows how the subjects relate to one another rather than looking at them as separate topics.

In the years after her retirement, Katherine
continued to spread the word about space far
and wide. She also continued writing. In 2002,
Katherine wrote a paper especially for teachers.
In it, Katherine offered ideas for how teachers
could hold space-science workshops in their
schools. Katherine's experience as a teacher
combined with her space-travel experience
made her the perfect candidate for the job.
The workshops would allow students to interact
with real scientists and engineers, helping grow
their love of science and math.

When asked in an interview what advice
she gives to students, Katherine said that she

stresses the importance of doing what you love, and always doing your best. These two pieces of advice were instilled in Katherine from a very young age. Her family and mentors had helped her achieve her dream of becoming a research mathematician by following these two rules. Katherine continues to "pay it forward," or pass along the favor, by inspiring young students today.

"**Follow** your **passion.** Whatever you're doing, do **your best** at **all times** and make it as correct as possible."

Katherine Johnson, 2018

Chapter

12

AWARDS AND **acclaim**

Katherine's family, friends, and colleagues knew how big her contribution to space flight was—but for a while, they were the only ones.

It wasn't until many years after Katherine's retirement at NASA that the rest of the world began to pay attention. Gradually Katherine's reputation grew, and she started to get the recognition she deserved. This reached its peak in 2015 when, at the age of 97, Katherine was given an extremely important award.

The White House,
Washington, D.C.

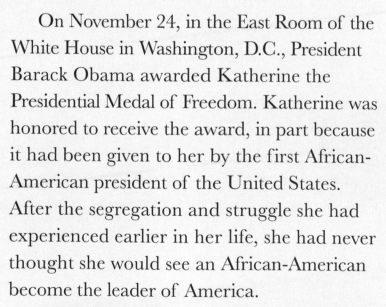

PRESIDENTIAL MEDAL OF FREEDOM

This medal is the United States' highest civilian honor. It is awarded by the President of the United States to a US citizen, and it recognizes those people who have made a very special contribution to society in some way.

On November 24, in the East Room of the White House in Washington, D.C., President Barack Obama awarded Katherine the Presidential Medal of Freedom. Katherine was honored to receive the award, in part because it had been given to her by the first African-American president of the United States. After the segregation and struggle she had experienced earlier in her life, she had never thought she would see an African-American become the leader of America.

Katherine's contributions to NASA were groundbreaking. They had come during a time of discrimination and prejudice against both African-Americans and women. Two months before the ceremony, in a speech to the Congressional Black Caucus, President Obama had said, "Black women have been a part of every great movement in American history, even if they weren't always given a voice."

That's what made Katherine's journey and recognition so momentous. African-American women have made significant contributions to the history of the United States, but not all of those stories have yet been heard. Receiving the Presidential Medal of Freedom gave the world an opportunity to listen to Katherine's influential story.

During the ceremony, President Obama read the diverse stories and accomplishments of all 17 of the people being given the award. Katherine was honored alongside artists, athletes, activists, and former members of the US military.

What is the Congressional Black Caucus?

A political organization made up of the African-American members of the United States Congress.

President Obama
awards Katherine
with the Presidential
Medal of Freedom.

103

After placing the medals around the necks of the recipients, the president said, "What a great blessing to be in a nation where individuals as diverse, from as wildly different backgrounds, can help to shape our dreams, how we live together, help define justice and freedom and love. They represent what's best in us, and we are very, very proud to be able to celebrate them here today."

Katherine has accepted many other awards in her lifetime—including NASA's Group Achievement Award, West Virginia State's Outstanding Alumnus of the Year, and many honorary degrees. However, she has said that receiving the Presidential Medal of Freedom was a moment that stood above the rest.

The following spring, NASA honored Katherine's work by dedicating a building at Langley to her. The Katherine G. Johnson

Computational Research Facility at NASA is about 37,000 ft² (3,400 m²) in size, and it cost $23 million to build.

The building's dedication ceremony took place on May 5, 2016, the 55th anniversary of Alan Shepard's space flight on *Freedom 7*. At the ceremony, the governor of Virginia called Katherine a "trailblazer." He also said that she had played an important part in the history of Virginia. Members of the community, NASA employees, and students were there to show

---

what is a trailblazer?

An inspiring person who does something that has never been done before, leading the way for other people.

their admiration for Katherine and her work. When asked about the building, Katherine joked that NASA was "crazy" for dedicating an entire building to her—but she may have been the only one who thought so! Katherine has always remained modest about her achievements, saying, "I was just doing my job."

Today, Katherine is retired from her work, but she is still busy. As well as spending time with her family, Katherine enjoys traveling, playing bridge, and watching sports.

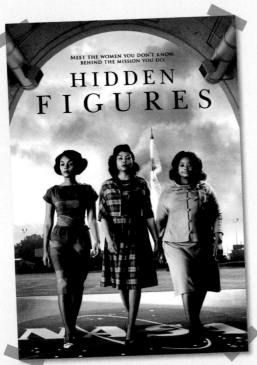

The movie *Hidden Figures* (2016) tells Katherine's story, as well as the stories of her coworkers Dorothy Vaughan and Mary Jackson. It is based on a book by the same name by Margot Lee Shetterly, which told the world how their work at NASA helped the US win the Space Race.

Katherine still speaks to students about her career and encourages them to pursue STEM careers. She tells them, "We will always have STEM with us. Some things will drop out of the public eye and will go away, but there will always be science, engineering, and technology. And there will always, always be mathematics."

DID YOU KNOW?

The movie *Hidden Figures* received nominations for three Academy Awards®.

Katherine was recently asked if she still counts things. She replied, "Oh, yes. And things have to be parallel. I see a picture right now that's not parallel, so I'm going to go straighten it. Things must be in order."

In an address to Hampton University graduates in 2017, Katherine offered some advice to those who wanted to follow in her footsteps: "Always do your best for whatever you're doing. Do your best. But enjoy it. Enjoy life. As it passes by you, don't miss anything." Katherine didn't just make up that advice—she lives it every moment of her life, all the way to present day.

Katherine's presence at NASA alone broke many barriers that existed for most women, especially African-American women, at the time. Her brilliant mind for math and her determined attitude helped put people on the moon. When the expectation was that women would do what they were told to do without asking questions, she did the opposite. Because of her courage, Katherine stood out—and in doing so, she changed the world.

Katherine's
family tree

Father

Joshua McKinley Coleman
1881–1973

Brother

Horace Coleman
1912–1950

Sister

Margaret Coleman
1913–2002

Brother

Charles Coleman
1915–2008

First husband

James Francis Goble
1913–1956

Daughter

Joylette Goble Hylick
1940–

110

Katherine's parents
married in 1909.

Mother

Joylette Roberta
Coleman
1887–1971

Katherine
Johnson

1918–

Second
husband

James A.
Johnson
1925–

Katherine married
James in 1959.

Constance
Goble Boykin
Garcia
1943–2010

Daughter

Katherine
Goble Moore
c.1944–

Daughter

Timeline

On August 26, Katherine is born in White Sulphur Springs, West Virginia.

Katherine graduates from college. Over the next few years, she teaches at schools in Virginia and West Virginia.

Katherine graduates from high school at age 14.

1918   1928   1932   1933   1937

Katherine moves to Institute, West Virginia, with her mother and siblings. There, she attends a high school for black students.

At 15, Katherine begins studying at West Virginia State, an all-black college.

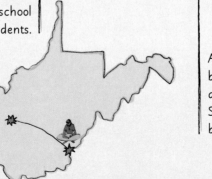

Katherine marries James Francis Goble. They go on to have three daughters—Joylette, Constance, and Katherine—before James dies of brain cancer in 1956.

NACA becomes NASA, and Katherine joins the Space Task Group. She works on Project Mercury, which aims to put a human in space.

1939

1953

1958

Katherine is one of the first three black students to attend West Virginia State's graduate program.

After several years of teaching, Katherine becomes a "human computer" at the National Advisory Committee for Aeronautics (NACA).

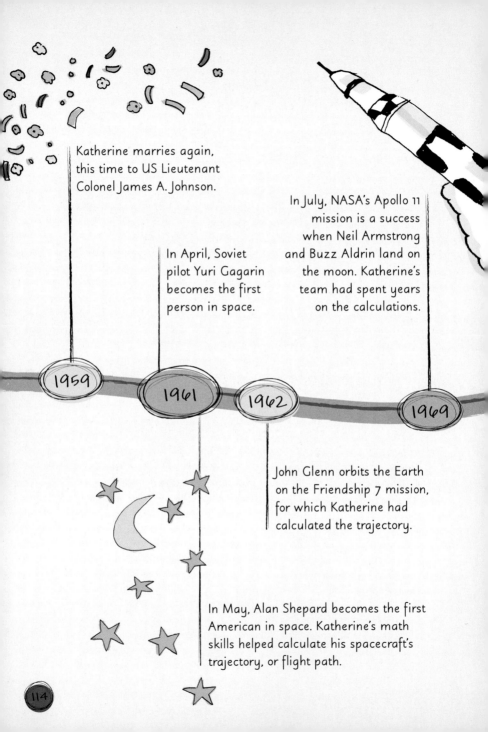

Katherine marries again, this time to US Lieutenant Colonel James A. Johnson.

In April, Soviet pilot Yuri Gagarin becomes the first person in space.

In July, NASA's Apollo 11 mission is a success when Neil Armstrong and Buzz Aldrin land on the moon. Katherine's team had spent years on the calculations.

1959

1961

1962

1969

John Glenn orbits the Earth on the Friendship 7 mission, for which Katherine had calculated the trajectory.

In May, Alan Shepard becomes the first American in space. Katherine's math skills helped calculate his spacecraft's trajectory, or flight path.

Katherine is awarded the Presidential Medal of Freedom in recognition of her groundbreaking work at NASA.

Katherine's career at NASA is covered in the book *Hidden Figures* by Margot Lee Shetterly. A movie based on the book is released, as well.

1986

2015

2016

Katherine retires from NASA after working there for 33 years.

NASA names a building in Katherine's honor. She attends the dedication ceremony with her family.

Quiz

 1. How many children did Joylette and Joshua Coleman have?

 2. Which musical instrument did Katherine learn to play in high school?

 3. Who introduced Katherine to the idea of working as a research mathematician?

 4. Which court ordered traditionally white colleges to admit black students?

 5. Where did James Goble work when he and Katherine lived in Newport News?

 6. What were the women who did calculations by hand at NASA called?

 7. To which 1958 report did Katherine contribute equations?

Do you remember what you've read? How many of these questions about Katherine's life can you answer?

8 What do the letters in NASA stand for?

9 On what date did Apollo 11 launch from the Kennedy Space Center in Florida?

10 For how many seconds did Michael Collins fire Apollo 11's engine to correct its trajectory?

11 For how many years had Katherine worked at NASA when she retired in 1986?

12 Which medal did Katherine receive at the White House in 2015?

Answers on page 128

Who's who?

Aldrin, Edwin ("Buzz")
(1930–) second person to walk on the moon

Armstrong, Neil
(1930–2012) first person to walk on the moon

Armstrong, W. O.
(Unknown) second black student to earn a master's degree at West Virginia State

Claytor, William
(1908–1967) math professor at West Virginia State

Coleman, Charles
(1915–2008) Katherine's older brother

Coleman, Horace
(1912–1950) Katherine's older brother

Coleman, Joshua McKinley
(1881–1973) Katherine's dad

Coleman, Joylette Roberta Lowe
(1887–1971) Katherine's mom

Coleman, Margaret
(1913–2002) Katherine's older sister

Collins, Michael
(1930–2012) command module pilot for Apollo 11

Davis, John W.
(1888–1980) president of West Virginia State from 1919 to 1953

Faget, Maxime
(1921–2004) spacecraft designer and member of the Space Task Group

Gagarin, Yuri
(1934–1968) Soviet pilot; first person to go into space

Garcia, Constance Goble
(1943–2010) Katherine's second daughter

Gilruth, Robert
(1913–2000) head of the Space Task Group

Glenn, John
(1921–2016) first American to orbit the Earth

Goble, James Francis
(1913–1956) Katherine's first husband

Gus, Sherman H.
(Unknown) Katherine's high-school principal

Haise, Fred
(1933–) Apollo 13 crew member

Hylick, Joylette Goble
(1940–) Katherine's oldest daughter

Jackson, Mary
(1921–2005) Katherine's colleague who became NASA's first black, female engineer

James, Kenneth
(Unknown) first black student to earn a master's degree at West Virginia State

Johnson, James A.
(1925–) Army colonel; Katherine's second husband

Kennedy, John F.
(1917–1963) president of the US from 1961 to 1963

King, Turner Angie
(1905–2004) Katherine's high school math teacher

Lovell, Jim
(1928–) Apollo 13 crew member

Moore, Katherine Goble
(c.1944–) Katherine's youngest daughter

Obama, Barack
(1961–) president of the US from 2009 to 2017

Roosevelt, Franklin D.
(1882–1945) president of the US from 1933 to 1945

Shepard, Alan
(1923–1998) first American in space

Shetterly, Margot Lee
(1969–) author of the book *Hidden Figures*

Swigert, Jack
(1931–1982) Apollo 13 crew member

Vaughan, Dorothy
(1910–2008) colleague of Katherine's who learned to program computers

Glossary

activist
someone who takes action against something he or she feels is wrong

advocacy
publicly supporting a certain person or a group

aeronautics
science of flight

artificial satellite
human-made device that travels around the Earth or another body in space, transmitting information

astronomy
study of the universe beyond the Earth, including space, solar systems, and galaxies

atmosphere
thick layer of gases around the Earth that protects it from the burning rays of the sun

colonel
senior-ranking officer in the US Army, Air Force, or Marines

command module
crew cabin of the Apollo 11 spacecraft, also serving as the capsule that brought the crew back to Earth

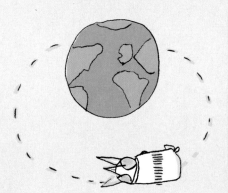

Congress
law-making branch of the US government

Congressional Black Caucus
political organization made up of the African-American members of the US Congress

constellation
group of stars forming a pattern in the night sky

discrimination
practice of treating one person or a group of people unfairly

geometry
math of shapes

graduation
receiving of an academic degree or diploma

gravity
force that causes physical objects to fall toward the Earth or any other body with mass

honorary
given as an honor, or out of respect, and without payment

honors
an award or symbol of excellence or superiority

human computer
person who calculates data and analyzes information

human error
mistake made by a person that causes the results of something to be wrong

integration
bringing people of different races together to make sure they are treated equally

launch window
exact moment when a spacecraft needs to take off to reach space

lunar materials
minerals and rocks found on the moon's surface

lunar module
part of the Apollo 11 spacecraft that landed on the moon

Mission Control
place on the Earth that houses the equipment and staff that control a spaceflight

navigational charts
star charts drawn up to help astronauts guide their spacecraft in case of emergency

orbit
path an object takes around another when pulled by its gravity

PhD
abbreviation that stands for "Doctor of Philosophy," which is an academic degree

research mathematician
someone who develops math theories and looks for trends in sets of data

rivalry
intense competition between two people or groups of people

sacrifice
action someone takes to give up something valuable for another or for the greater good

segregation
keeping people of
different races or
religions separate
from each other

service module
part of the Apollo 11
spacecraft that powered
its flight

sorority
female-only social club
at a college or university

Soviet Union
former country that
spread across Eastern
Europe and northern
Asia, made up of Russia
and 14 other states,
between 1922 and 1991

splashdown
"landing" of a space
capsule, assisted
by parachutes,
on the ocean

substitute teacher
teacher who leads a class
when the regular teacher
is away

Supreme Court
the highest court in
the United States

throttle
to control the flow
of fuel to an engine

trailblazer
inspiring person who
does something that
has never been done
before, leading the
way for others

trajectory
path an object follows
through air or space

turbulence
sudden, violent
movements experienced
by flying aircraft due
to changes in the air

Index

Acknowledgments

DK would like to thank: Romi Chakraborty and Pallavi Narain for design support; Lindsay Walter-Greaney for proofreading; Hilary Bird for the index; Emily Kimball and Nishani Reed for legal advice; and Jamor Gaffney and Stephanie Laird for consulting.

The publisher would like to thank the following for their kind permission to reproduce their photographs:
(Key: a-above; b-below/bottom; c-center; f-far; l-left; r-right; t-top)

23 Alamy Stock Photo: Backyard Productions. 29 Dreamstime.com: Jim Pickerell (tr). 37 Getty Images: Bloomberg. 39 Getty Images: Alfred Eisenstaedt / The LIFE Picture Collection. 43 Getty Images: Stocktrek Images. 44 Dorling Kindersley: Gary Ombler / Gatwick Aviation Museum. 46 Alamy Stock Photo: PJF Military Collection. 48 NASA: JPL-Caltech. 51 NASA. 59 NASA: Langley Research Center (cla, cr, bl). 60 NASA. 62 NASA. 63 NASA: (cra, bl). 64 NASA. 65 NASA: Langley Research Center. 68 Alamy Stock Photo: Trinity Mirror / Mirrorpix. 70–71 NASA. 73 NASA. 76 NASA. 78–79 Getty Images: Ralph Crane / The LIFE Picture Collection. 84 NASA: MSFC. 85 NASA. 87 NASA: MSFC. 89 NASA. 90–91 NASA.

93 Getty Images: Time Life Pictures / NASA / The LIFE Picture Collection. 100 Dreamstime.com: Alberto Dubini / Dolby1985. 103 Getty Images: Kris Connor / WireImage. 106 Alamy Stock Photo: © Levantine Films / Entertainment Pictures / ZUMAPRESS.com. 109 NASA. 111 NASA: (cr)

Cover images: Front: Alamy Stock Photo: NASA Archive; Spine: Alamy Stock Photo: NASA Archive

All other images © Dorling Kindersley
For further information see: www.dkimages.com

ANSWERS TO THE QUIZ ON PAGES 116–117

1. four children; 2. piano; 3. Dr. Claytor, her professor; 4. US Supreme Court; 5. Newport News shipyard; 6. human computers; 7. "Notes on Space Technology"; 8. National Aeronautics and Space Administration; 9. July 16, 1969; 10. three seconds; 11. 33 years; 12. Presidential Medal of Freedom